I AM
Woman

DEVOTIONAL FOR ELEVATED LIVING

I AM
Woman

DEVOTIONAL FOR ELEVATED LIVING

SYLVIA HIGH

MYND
MATTERS

Books may be purchased in quantity and/or special sales by contacting the author.

Published by
Mynd Matters Publishing
715 Peachtree Street NE, Suites 100 & 200
Atlanta, GA 30308
www.myndmatterspublishing.com

978-1-948145-58-9

FIRST EDITION

Introduction

Women are the most powerful beings on the planet. We are the only beings, other than God, that can create another human and that is powerful. Yet historically, we have allowed the pre-determined definition of what it means to be woman to define us, to tell us who we are, how we should act, what we should say, how we should feel, and what we should desire or dream.

Society is a powerful force that has set boundaries and limitations on us. Instead of defining our own roles, we allowed the role of woman to be defined by others, based on external factors such as geography, culture, education, sibling order, societal norms, and so much more.

Even if you have taken the time to answer the questions, Who am I as a woman? What does it mean to me to **be** a woman?

There is always more!

The truth is, women are the salt of the earth. Yes, we are natural healers and it's in our DNA to nurture and to take care of those around us. However, we are so much more. We are also creators, innovators, leaders, trailblazers, forerunners, and game changers.

We are powerful. We are beyond measure. We are unlimited.

There is *NO thing* we cannot accomplish.

That is why the *I Am Woman Devotional for Elevated Living* was written, to be your companion. To serve as a catalyst to inspire you to discover and own ALL of who you are.

It is a journey that demands you to define who you are—to get clear about what you value and what matters to you. The woman you are *today*. Not the woman someone else told you to be, not even the woman you decided you were some years ago, or even one year ago.

If you are reading this book, I am beyond thrilled for you and all that will open up. The inspiration, challenges, revelations, renewal, reset, and full ownership of who you are and all that it means to be one of the most powerful forces on the planet.

God made us as pure possibilities with the gift to transform, shift, and grow until we are no longer here on earth. I even think it continues afterwards.

The question I am asking you to answer in many ways is, *Who are you? Why are you? What are you?*

If you knew you could not fail, what would you be doing, saying, contributing, and creating? How would you change the world?

What I know for sure is you matter, you are amazing, and you deserve all that your heart desires.

What does your heart desire? What matters that you have not yet accomplished? What would have you jump out of bed each morning filled with excitement and joy? What if you 110% own the truth about you?

You are amazing, brilliant, and incredible. Every dream and idea that you have has been placed in you deliberately—a unique gift for you, to you, that only you can fulfill and all that you need to fulfill it came with you. It is built into who you are. You simply need to discover what part of yourself is in the way.

So, let's get busy!

The way to get the most out of the *I Am Woman Devotional* is to do it daily. I love early mornings and late evenings, but any time you choose will evoke amazing, life-changing insights. Remember, you deserve the gift of daily renewal to avoid pouring from an empty cup. You are fulfilling the dreams that matter to you and to the world.

How Best To Use This Devotional:

Each page is designed to expose more of you to you. Allow yourself the freedom to let whatever comes up, come out. Challenge yourself to be emotionally honest and say the things you'd rather not. Similarly, be generous in acknowledging your gifts and your worth as you reflect.

Included are 45 unique Distinctions. For each Distinction, there is an empowering truth and a declaration. Once you declare the statement, jot down what comes to mind. Write down how the distinction and declaration will manifest in your life. Finally, answer the two questions to clarify what denying the truth has or will cost you and then what possibilities are unlocked when you own the truth.

Your expanded, transformed self is waiting for you. She is excited to take new ground and I am excited to take it with you.

Thank you for joining me on the journey of ELEVATION!

Unlimited

I am Woman, therefore, I am unlimited.

There's no extent to which I cannot go,
Beyond the moon, stars, galaxies.

I am unlimited, far reaching, boundless,
Inexhaustible, endless, untold, measureless,
Incalculable, vast, immense, great.

God made me immeasurable so that every desire, dream, inkling,
wish, hope, yearning, longing is mine to fulfill.

TRUTH: I AM UNLIMITED

I Am Woman, therefore, I Am Unlimited:

_____

_____

_____

_____

_____

_____

_____

_____

_____

_____

_____

_____

_____

_____

_____

_____

_____

_____

_____

Denying This Truth Has/Will Cost Me:

_____

_____

_____

_____

_____

_____

_____

_____

_____

_____

_____

_____

_____

_____

_____

_____

By Owning This Truth What Becomes Possible Is:

_____

_____

_____

_____

_____

_____

_____

_____

_____

_____

_____

_____

_____

_____

_____

_____

_____

_____

_____

Magnificent

I am Woman, therefore, I am magnificent.

I am magnificent, splendid, spectacular, impressive, striking, glorious, superb, majestic, awesome.

The magnificence of who I am is so brilliant that it is blinding to the eye, Impossible to behold or capture.

By embracing the divinity of what it means to be woman, it gives me access to bask in the glory of God's image within me.

I am Woman and I am magnificent.

TRUTH: I AM SPLENDID AND MAGNIFICENT

I Am Woman, therefore, I Am Magnificent:

_____

_____

_____

_____

_____

_____

_____

_____

_____

_____

_____

_____

_____

_____

_____

_____

_____

Denying This Truth Has/Will Cost Me:

_____

_____

_____

_____

_____

_____

_____

_____

_____

_____

_____

_____

_____

_____

_____

_____

_____

_____

By Owning This Truth What Becomes Possible Is:

Light

I am Woman, therefore, I am light.

I am light, radiant, I am the flame, I am the source of light,
I and God almighty are one therefore,
darkness cannot exist in the radiance of my presence.

My brilliance and glow cause all that is not light and good to
dissipate.

When God made woman, he purposed me.

Built into my very existence the power to bring light to every dark
place, circumstance or situation.

As Woman, I have the gift to illuminate that which would not be
illuminated.

TRUTH: I AM ILLUMINATION

I Am Woman, therefore, I Am Light:

_____

_____

_____

_____

_____

_____

_____

_____

_____

_____

_____

_____

_____

_____

_____

_____

_____

_____

_____

Denying This Truth Has/Will Cost Me:

_____

_____

_____

_____

_____

_____

_____

_____

_____

_____

_____

_____

_____

_____

_____

_____

_____

_____

_____

By Owning This Truth What Becomes Possible Is:

I Matter

I am Woman, therefore, I matter.

I matter. I am important, significant, relevant. I carry weight.

I am purposeful—there is nothing about me that is accidental or coincidental.

I have a voice, a point of view, a perspective.

I am distinct, a contribution.

I have something to say. What I have to say is important.

I am to be heard, listened to, respected, acknowledged.

I shall **not** be discarded, ignored, devalued or diminished.

I am whole, perfect, and complete.

I am divine.

TRUTH: I AM VALUABLE

I Am Woman, therefore, I Matter:

_____

_____

_____

_____

_____

_____

_____

_____

_____

_____

_____

_____

_____

_____

_____

_____

_____

_____

_____

Denying This Truth Has/Will Cost Me:

_____

_____

_____

_____

_____

_____

_____

_____

_____

_____

_____

_____

_____

_____

_____

_____

_____

By Owning This Truth What Becomes Possible Is:

_____

_____

_____

_____

_____

_____

_____

_____

_____

_____

_____

_____

_____

_____

_____

_____

_____

_____

Innovative

I am Woman, therefore, I am innovative.

I bring change and create anew.

I am innovative, novel, fresh, unconventional, unorthodox, unusual, unfamiliar, unprecedented, avant-garde, experimental, inventive, ingenious, advanced, futuristic, a pioneer, ground-breaking, a trail blazer, revolutionary, radical, disruptive, new-fangled, new fashioned.

I am Woman—I am what hasn't happened yet, what is to come, and all there is to be.

God gave me the ability to imagine and create beyond what is.

I am innovative and creative in my thinking and power and given the ability to see all there is to come and beyond.

I am here to create. I am purpose-fulfilled, purpose manifested.

I am state of the art.

TRUTH: I AM A CREATIVE AND INNOVATIVE

I Am Woman, therefore, I Am Innovative:

_____

_____

_____

_____

_____

_____

_____

_____

_____

_____

_____

_____

_____

_____

_____

_____

_____

_____

Denying This Truth Has/Will Cost Me:

_____

_____

_____

_____

_____

_____

_____

_____

_____

_____

_____

_____

_____

_____

_____

_____

_____

_____

By Owning This Truth What Becomes Possible Is:

_____

_____

_____

_____

_____

_____

_____

_____

_____

_____

_____

_____

_____

_____

_____

_____

_____

_____

Intuitive

I am Woman, therefore, I am intuitive.

Intuition is the ability to understand something immediately without the need of conscious reasoning.

It is the part of me that divinely knows,
it is my connection to my divinity.

I am intuitive, pure spirit, unfiltered truth.

Intuition is the voice of God from which all answers are revealed.

My intuition is my inner guide, the Holy Spirit that will take me beyond mind, visible, tangible, evidence or proof.

It is wisdom.

My duty is to listen, trust, obey and manifest all the gifts that are being revealed through my intuition.

It is the voice of God saying listen to me my daughter.

TRUTH: I AM DIVINE INTUITION

I Am Woman, therefore, I Am Intuitive:

_____

_____

_____

_____

_____

_____

_____

_____

_____

_____

_____

_____

_____

_____

_____

_____

_____

_____

Denying This Truth Has/Will Cost Me:

_____

_____

_____

_____

_____

_____

_____

_____

_____

_____

_____

_____

_____

_____

_____

_____

_____

_____

By Owning This Truth What Becomes Possible Is:

_____

_____

_____

_____

_____

_____

_____

_____

_____

_____

_____

_____

_____

_____

_____

_____

_____

_____

Free

I am Woman, therefore, I am free.

Freedom is the state of not being imprisoned or enslaved.

The power or right to act, speak or think as one wants without
hindrance or restraint.

I am Woman; independent; self-determined; sovereign;
emancipated; liberated; delivered; non-confirming; an individual.

I have attained manumission,
which means to be released from slavery.

I am to honor, cherish and guard the gift of my freedom with all of
my being.

Speaking what I choose, speaking my truth, walking my truth.

**TRUTH: I AM FREE, LIBERATED, AND
EMANCIPATED FROM ALL BONDAGE**

I Am Woman, therefore, I Am Free:

_____

_____

_____

_____

_____

_____

_____

_____

_____

_____

_____

_____

_____

_____

_____

_____

_____

_____

_____

Denying This Truth Has/Will Cost Me:

_____

_____

_____

_____

_____

_____

_____

_____

_____

_____

_____

_____

_____

_____

_____

_____

_____

_____

By Owning This Truth What Becomes Possible Is:

_____

_____

_____

_____

_____

_____

_____

_____

_____

_____

_____

_____

_____

_____

_____

_____

_____

_____

Grace

I am Woman, therefore, I am grace.

I am grace—refined, elegant, effortless, poised, finesse,
dignified, distinguished.

Not only am I grace, I am graceful.

I overflow with God's generosity empowering me to impart
strength, healing, compassion, and love.

When I bestow grace upon humanity,
that same grace is imparted upon me.

TRUTH: I AM GRACE

I Am Woman, therefore, I Am Grace:

_____

_____

_____

_____

_____

_____

_____

_____

_____

_____

_____

_____

_____

_____

_____

_____

_____

_____

Denying This Truth Has/Will Cost Me:

_____

_____

_____

_____

_____

_____

_____

_____

_____

_____

_____

_____

_____

_____

_____

_____

_____

_____

_____

By Owning This Truth What Becomes Possible Is:

_____

_____

_____

_____

_____

_____

_____

_____

_____

_____

_____

_____

_____

_____

_____

_____

_____

_____

_____

Responsible

I am Woman, therefore, I am responsible.

I have the power and ability to respond.

I am boundless, powerful beyond measure,
a force to be reckoned with.

God has given each of his daughters the power and ability to respond any time, any place, about anything.

However, we so often allow the world's definition of *Woman* to arrest and hold us captive.

The world defines *Woman* telling her who she should be, what she should do, what she should say, and how she should show up— characterizing her, squeezing her, into a box that is far too small for who God designed her to be.

In fact, God says we are not to be boxed in.

We are not to allow the world to dictate how we occur.

We must say no to oppression, depression, omission, shrinkage, belittlement, invisibility, muting or condescension.

TRUTH: I AM RESPONSE-ABLE

I Am Woman, therefore, I Am Responsible:

_____

_____

_____

_____

_____

_____

_____

_____

_____

_____

_____

_____

_____

_____

_____

_____

_____

_____

Denying This Truth Has/Will Cost Me:

_____

_____

_____

_____

_____

_____

_____

_____

_____

_____

_____

_____

_____

_____

_____

_____

_____

_____

By Owning This Truth What Becomes Possible Is:

_____

_____

_____

_____

_____

_____

_____

_____

_____

_____

_____

_____

_____

_____

_____

_____

_____

_____

_____

Wind

I am Woman, therefore, I am the wind.

The great Toni Morrison said it best, "If you surrender to the wind, you can ride it."

I am transcended, elevated, and sky-rocketed beyond the pull of life's conditions, mindsets, or opinions.

By surrendering to the wind, it elevates me above all of life's circumstances, heartaches, pain, disappointment, adversity, challenges and discouragement.

I am Woman.

I soar the way God designed me to, above all things.

Nothing can hold me captive.

TRUTH: I AM WIND

I Am Woman, therefore, I Am the Wind:

_____

_____

_____

_____

_____

_____

_____

_____

_____

_____

_____

_____

_____

_____

_____

_____

_____

_____

Denying This Truth Has/Will Cost Me:

_____

_____

_____

_____

_____

_____

_____

_____

_____

_____

_____

_____

_____

_____

_____

_____

_____

By Owning This Truth What Becomes Possible Is:

_____

_____

_____

_____

_____

_____

_____

_____

_____

_____

_____

_____

_____

_____

_____

_____

_____

_____

Excite

I am Woman, therefore, I am excited.

Excite means to cause strong feelings of enthusiasm.
It is eagerness.

It brings about a rise. It electrifies. It is provocative and
stimulating. It kindles and causes.

As *Women*, we are a powerful force. It is imperative that we are
intentional and consistent about the attitude and state of mind we
bring to our daily lives.

It is our state of mind that determines our experience
and quality of life.

Not only does our attitude determine the quality of our experience
in life, we've all heard the cliché that one's
"attitude determines their altitude."

Except it's not just a cliché.

It drives the actions we take and the actions we take determine
and create the very outcomes of our lives.

TRUTH: ATTITUDE MATTERS

I Am Woman, therefore, I Am Excited:

Denying This Truth Has/Will Cost Me:

_____

_____

_____

_____

_____

_____

_____

_____

_____

_____

_____

_____

_____

_____

_____

_____

_____

By Owning This Truth What Becomes Possible Is:

_____

_____

_____

_____

_____

_____

_____

_____

_____

_____

_____

_____

_____

_____

_____

_____

_____

_____

Rhythm

I am Woman, therefore, I am rhythm.

My rhythm is unique to me.

My heart has a beat. I have a pace, swag, sway, movement, sound,
tempo, cadence—that make me uniquely me.

When I honor my rhythm, I am in sync with the music of my soul.

When I am in sync with the music of my soul,
I can dance the dance of my spirit.

When I can dance the dance of my spirit, the angels rejoice.

There is no denying that I am a divine design.

My heartbeat is the pulse of God.

TRUTH: I AM RHYTHM

I Am Woman, therefore, I Am Rhythm:

_____

_____

_____

_____

_____

_____

_____

_____

_____

_____

_____

_____

_____

_____

_____

_____

_____

_____

Denying This Truth Has/Will Cost Me:

_____

_____

_____

_____

_____

_____

_____

_____

_____

_____

_____

_____

_____

_____

_____

_____

_____

By Owning This Truth What Becomes Possible Is:

_____

_____

_____

_____

_____

_____

_____

_____

_____

_____

_____

_____

_____

_____

_____

_____

_____

_____

Renew

I am Woman, therefore, I am renewed.

"Morning by morning, new mercies appear."

Morning by morning, I am a blank canvas.

Each and every day, I am an unlimited possibility with the incredible gift to recreate or create anew.

As Woman, I have the ability and power to interrupt and redesign again, and again, and again.

Yesterday has no impact or bearing on my today unless I give it permission.

Stop, look, and notice where you are allowing your yesterdays to influence, impact, and limit your todays, and ultimately, your tomorrows.

The price is high and it is contrary to the power God gave you in the way he designed you.

Starting now as a practice, renew again, again, and again, and enjoy the fresh perspective and experience of what it means to live renewed.

TRUTH: I AM RENEWABLE

I Am Woman, therefore, I Am Renewable:

_____

_____

_____

_____

_____

_____

_____

_____

_____

_____

_____

_____

_____

_____

_____

_____

_____

_____

_____

Denying This Truth Has/Will Cost Me:

_____

_____

_____

_____

_____

_____

_____

_____

_____

_____

_____

_____

_____

_____

_____

_____

_____

_____

By Owning This Truth What Becomes Possible Is:

_____

_____

_____

_____

_____

_____

_____

_____

_____

_____

_____

_____

_____

_____

_____

_____

_____

Release

I am Woman, therefore, I can release.

I release all that doesn't serve me.

To release means to escape from confinement, to set free,
To move, act or flow freely.

When we do not release, when we are unwilling to let go,
we find ourselves living a life that has expired.

Living a life that has expired, keeps us stuck in relationships,
careers, habits, beliefs, and perspectives
that no longer serve or empower.

As Woman, I have the power to let go, set free, flow, and be
released from all that I have allowed to confine me.

Today, I release.

TRUTH: I RELEASE

I Am Woman, therefore, I Release:

_____

_____

_____

_____

_____

_____

_____

_____

_____

_____

_____

_____

_____

_____

_____

_____

_____

_____

Denying This Truth Has/Will Cost Me:

_____

_____

_____

_____

_____

_____

_____

_____

_____

_____

_____

_____

_____

_____

_____

_____

_____

_____

By Owning This Truth What Becomes Possible Is:

_____

_____

_____

_____

_____

_____

_____

_____

_____

_____

_____

_____

_____

_____

_____

_____

_____

_____

Fun

I am Woman, therefore, I am fun.

Fun means amusement, enjoyment, and light-hearted pleasure.

As Woman, so much of our predominant role is to heal, nurture, be caregivers, and provide for our families, communities, careers, and relationships. So much that we often forget to give to ourselves or permit ourselves to receive.

While we've taken on all of these roles whole-heartedly, a great part of who we are is the little girl who just wants to have fun.

Remember each day to be mindful, to restore yourself daily by intentionally creating a fun experience.

Whether it is five minutes, ten minutes, or an entire day of fun, give yourself permission to be the little girl that just wants to have fun!

TRUTH: I AM FOREVER WOMAN AND I AM FOREVER GIRL

I Am Woman, therefore, I Am Fun:

_____

_____

_____

_____

_____

_____

_____

_____

_____

_____

_____

_____

_____

_____

_____

_____

_____

_____

Denying This Truth Has/Will Cost Me:

_____

_____

_____

_____

_____

_____

_____

_____

_____

_____

_____

_____

_____

_____

_____

_____

_____

_____

By Owning This Truth What Becomes Possible Is:

_____

_____

_____

_____

_____

_____

_____

_____

_____

_____

_____

_____

_____

_____

_____

_____

_____

_____

Integrous

I am Woman, therefore, I am integrous.
Integrity is one of my fundamental values.
I am honest, I am strong.
I am upright, I am sincere.
I am trustworthy, I am whole.

I am steady.
I am good, decent.
I am honorable, I am solid.
I say what I mean, I mean what I say.
I don't go along to get along.

I refuse to dilute who I am by pretending, acquiescing, or giving
in to anything that is not my truth.
I am *Woman* and my integrity is non-negotiable.
I know that my integrity is at a high price. It determines
fundamentally who I am.
It is my foundation.

When I compromise my integrity, it robs me of my credibility,
trust, and power with the most important person—myself.
Being integrous, I become a person who I admire.
It is central, it is core.

TRUTH: "TO THINE OWN SELF BE TRUE."
—SOCRATES

I Am Woman, therefore, I Have Integrity:

_____

_____

_____

_____

_____

_____

_____

_____

_____

_____

_____

_____

_____

_____

_____

_____

_____

_____

_____

Denying This Truth Has/Will Cost Me:

_____

_____

_____

_____

_____

_____

_____

_____

_____

_____

_____

_____

_____

_____

_____

_____

_____

By Owning This Truth What Becomes Possible Is:

_____

_____

_____

_____

_____

_____

_____

_____

_____

_____

_____

_____

_____

_____

_____

_____

_____

_____

Transforming

I am Woman, therefore, I am transforming.

I am always transforming to something and from something.

I am Woman.

I can't be confined or defined, restricted or limited.

I am Woman and I am transformation, reshaping, remodeling, reconstructing, reworking, renewing, renovating.

I am Woman and I am unlimitedly living in a constant state of metamorphosis in this journey called life.

Morning-by-morning I am a new possibility.

I am Woman.

I am transformation.

TRUTH: I AM THE BOMB.COM

I Am Woman, therefore, I Am Transforming:

_____

_____

_____

_____

_____

_____

_____

_____

_____

_____

_____

_____

_____

_____

_____

_____

_____

_____

_____

Denying This Truth Has/Will Cost Me:

By Owning This Truth What Becomes Possible Is:

Action

I am Woman, therefore, I am action.

I am enterprising. I am engaged. I am accomplished.
I am an initiator.

I am movement. I am responsive. I am responsible. I am causing.
I'm a driver.

I am Woman and I am in action.

Not only am I in action, I am mindful that my actions align with
my visions.

My action forwards me, propels me.

My actions lift, create, drive, move, and manifest that which has
not happened yet.

I am Woman. Therefore, I take massive, bold actions that only
align with my vision.

It is only in action that I am able to turn my dreams into reality.

Action is the fuel and the catalyst to the life I dream about.

It brings the dream to life.

TRUTH: I AM WOMAN AND I AM ACTION

I Am Woman, therefore, I Am Action:

_____

_____

_____

_____

_____

_____

_____

_____

_____

_____

_____

_____

_____

_____

_____

_____

_____

Denying This Truth Has/Will Cost Me:

_____

_____

_____

_____

_____

_____

_____

_____

_____

_____

_____

_____

_____

_____

_____

_____

_____

_____

By Owning This Truth What Becomes Possible Is:

_____

_____

_____

_____

_____

_____

_____

_____

_____

_____

_____

_____

_____

_____

_____

_____

_____

_____

Leader

I am Woman, therefore, I am a leader.

A leader is a person who leads or commands a group, organization, or country.

I am Woman and I am a master, director, captain, governor, premier, guide, trailblazer, pacesetter, pathfinder, light bearer, initiator, developer, discoverer, and originator.

I am Woman.

I am leader. If it's to be, it's up to me.

As Woman, built into my psyche is a knowing without knowing. I hold the ability to anticipate that which is to come and the sensitivity to know exactly what's needed when it is needed, where it is needed, and how it is needed. As a Woman, leader is a natural part of my feminine DNA.

In fact, when women rule the world, war will no longer be.

TRUTH: THE WORLD IS A DEMAND FOR MY LEADERSHIP

I Am Woman, therefore, I Am the Leader:

_____

_____

_____

_____

_____

_____

_____

_____

_____

_____

_____

_____

_____

_____

_____

_____

_____

_____

_____

Denying This Truth Has/Will Cost Me:

_____

_____

_____

_____

_____

_____

_____

_____

_____

_____

_____

_____

_____

_____

_____

_____

_____

_____

By Owning This Truth What Becomes Possible Is:

_____

_____

_____

_____

_____

_____

_____

_____

_____

_____

_____

_____

_____

_____

_____

_____

_____

Supreme

I am Woman, therefore, I am supreme.

I reign.

I am remarkable, incredible, outstanding, incomparable, and unparalleled. I am strong, intense, great, surpassing, and exceptional.

I am Woman and I reign over all that God has made.

There's nothing that I cannot achieve that I put my mind to.

My very purpose for being is to elevate humanity, the environment, and the world as we know it.

My assignment is to live supremely, so all that encounter me know it is possible for them also.

I am Woman. Therefore, it is my duty, my obligation, and my privilege to have been given the assignment by God to advance humanity spiritually, emotionally, and financially.

In other words, to exalt and exhort.

TRUTH: I AM SUPREME

I Am Woman, therefore, I Am Supreme:

_____

_____

_____

_____

_____

_____

_____

_____

_____

_____

_____

_____

_____

_____

_____

_____

_____

_____

Denying This Truth Has/Will Cost Me:

_____

_____

_____

_____

_____

_____

_____

_____

_____

_____

_____

_____

_____

_____

_____

_____

By Owning This Truth What Becomes Possible Is:

_____

_____

_____

_____

_____

_____

_____

_____

_____

_____

_____

_____

_____

_____

_____

_____

_____

_____

_____

Water

I am Woman, therefore, I am water.

I am transparent. Like water, I am endless.

Like a spring, I forward others.

I am the river, I am sea.

There's no beginning, no end to who I am.

Like a pond, I'm a comforter.

I am ocean and it is impossible to be in my presence and not feel energized and called forth.

I am brilliant.

I am flow.

I am the force that moves others.

I am fresh and a refresher.

I am a force. I bring life. I bring vitality, strength, vibrancy, and I am a quencher.

I satisfy and revitalize that which has lost its vitality.

TRUTH: I AM ENDLESS

I Am Woman, therefore, I Am Water:

_____

_____

_____

_____

_____

_____

_____

_____

_____

_____

_____

_____

_____

_____

_____

_____

_____

_____

Denying This Truth Has/Will Cost Me:

_____

_____

_____

_____

_____

_____

_____

_____

_____

_____

_____

_____

_____

_____

_____

_____

_____

_____

By Owning This Truth What Becomes Possible Is:

_____

_____

_____

_____

_____

_____

_____

_____

_____

_____

_____

_____

_____

_____

_____

_____

_____

_____

No-thing

I am Woman, therefore, I am no-thing and I am everything.

I am Earth, I am sun, I am moon, and I am the stars.

I am wind. I am water. I am light.

I am Woman. I am man. I am child.

I am one with all there is and shall be.

I am vast, the creator and creation.

I am a resting place, a launching pad.

I am restoration as Woman.

I am spiritual.

I transcend.

TRUTH: I AM NO-THING

I Am Woman, therefore, I Am No-thing:

_____

_____

_____

_____

_____

_____

_____

_____

_____

_____

_____

_____

_____

_____

_____

_____

_____

Denying This Truth Has/Will Cost Me:

_____

_____

_____

_____

_____

_____

_____

_____

_____

_____

_____

_____

_____

_____

_____

_____

_____

By Owning This Truth What Becomes Possible Is:

_____

_____

_____

_____

_____

_____

_____

_____

_____

_____

_____

_____

_____

_____

_____

_____

_____

_____

_____

Willing

I am Woman, therefore, I am willing.

I am ready. I am eager. I am inclined.

I am agreeable, accommodating, enthusiastic.

I am giving.

I am Woman and I have a willing mind, heart, and spirit.

I am open and my open heart is the key to opening doors
and new possibilities.

As Woman, my willing spirit is a magnet that draws blessings and
also gives me the opportunity to be a blessing.

When I am willing, it gives me the ability to shift, release,
and let go of people, things, and history that does not serve my
greater good.

By being willing, it opens doors to discovery and to discovering,
learning, growing, and adventures that would not be available to a
closed heart.

When I am willing, I am actually saying yes to the unlimited gifts,
experiences, and evolution of my highest self.

TRUTH: I AM WOMAN AND I AM WILLING

I Am Woman, therefore, I Am Willing:

_____

_____

_____

_____

_____

_____

_____

_____

_____

_____

_____

_____

_____

_____

_____

_____

_____

Denying This Truth Has/Will Cost Me:

_____

_____

_____

_____

_____

_____

_____

_____

_____

_____

_____

_____

_____

_____

_____

_____

_____

_____

By Owning This Truth What Becomes Possible Is:

_____

_____

_____

_____

_____

_____

_____

_____

_____

_____

_____

_____

_____

_____

_____

_____

_____

_____

_____

Believe

I am Woman, therefore, I believe.
In that which I believe, I become.

To believe means to be convinced, to regard as true; to feel sure, to
imagine, to feel, to presume assume, conclude
When God gave women the gift of belief, embodied in the gift of belief is
freedom, expansion, limitlessness and pure possibility
On the other hand, if I am not intentional about how I use the power of
belief, this very gift can be confining, constricting,
oppressing and limiting.

As Woman, I have the right to choose what I believe.
Not only do I have the right to choose what I believe, I can, at any point
in time, redesign any belief that does not align, empower, inspire, or lift
me to the greatest version of myself.

Just like I update my technology, my cars, my jobs, my appliances, it is
imperative that I continue and continuously update my personal
operating systems, which are my beliefs.

My beliefs determine if I'm open or closed,
if I'm successful or unsuccessful.
They are the very core that ultimately determine
the quality of my life.

Negative beliefs create negative experiences. Positive powerful
forwarding beliefs create positive experiences, positives outcomes,
and a positive life.

In that which I believe, I become.

TRUTH: WHAT YOU BELIEVE MATTERS

I Am Woman, therefore, I Believe:

_____

_____

_____

_____

_____

_____

_____

_____

_____

_____

_____

_____

_____

_____

_____

_____

_____

_____

_____

Denying This Truth Has/Will Cost Me:

By Owning This Truth What Becomes Possible Is:

_____

_____

_____

_____

_____

_____

_____

_____

_____

_____

_____

_____

_____

_____

_____

_____

_____

_____

_____

Extraordinary

I am Woman, therefore, I am extraordinary.
I am remarkable, I am unusual, and I am exceptional.
I am an amazing, astounding, astonishing, and marvelous Woman.
I am wonderful and sensational, incredible, phenomenal.
I am extra-ordinarily designed to create the extraordinary.
There are over 7 billion people on the planet and over half are women
but none like me.

I am tremendous and fantastic.
I am too grand to encompass.
When God made me, He threw away the blueprint.
I am stupendous and awesome.
I am wondrous and ginormous.

I am extraordinary. I was born this great to accomplish great things.
I am indeed extraordinary, sent to contribute to the extraordinary.
Because I am extraordinary, I will invent what has not yet been
invented.

I will write what hasn't been written.
As Woman, I am extraordinary, therefore, I can bring forth to the planet
what eyes have not seen, ears have not heard.
My very purpose here on earth is to inspire, to stretch, to challenge, to
interrupt the status quo.

I am spectacular, noteworthy, and uncanny.
One might find me odd and peculiar.
I am so extraordinary the world will have to catch up to where I am to
have even a glimpse of my extra-ordinary-ness.

TRUTH: I AM EXTRAORDINARY

I Am Woman, therefore, I Am Extraordinary:

_____

_____

_____

_____

_____

_____

_____

_____

_____

_____

_____

_____

_____

_____

_____

_____

_____

Denying This Truth Has/Will Cost Me:

_____

_____

_____

_____

_____

_____

_____

_____

_____

_____

_____

_____

_____

_____

_____

_____

_____

_____

By Owning This Truth What Becomes Possible Is:

_____

_____

_____

_____

_____

_____

_____

_____

_____

_____

_____

_____

_____

_____

_____

_____

_____

_____

_____

_____

Beautiful

I am Woman, therefore, I am beautiful.

I am lovely, gorgeous, stunning, irresistible, exquisite, elegant, graceful, smashing, glamorous.

I am Woman and I am art.

Just as Michelangelo chiseled and created the masterpiece *David*, the greatest sculpture of all time, God himself, chiseled and made me the masterpiece that I am.

I am the ultimate definition of beauty.

God made me flawless because even my flaws are purposeful.

My flaws are not only my distinctions,
though they make me distinct.

When I embrace my beauty and see myself through God's eyes,
I shine so brightly that my rays are all-consuming.

While my outer beauty is exquisite, it is my inner beauty that makes me magnificent.

I am Woman and I am beautiful.

TRUTH: I AM WOMAN, I AM SPLENDID

I Am Woman, therefore, I Am Beautiful:

_____

_____

_____

_____

_____

_____

_____

_____

_____

_____

_____

_____

_____

_____

_____

_____

_____

_____

_____

_____

Denying This Truth Has/Will Cost Me:

_____

_____

_____

_____

_____

_____

_____

_____

_____

_____

_____

_____

_____

_____

_____

_____

_____

By Owning This Truth What Becomes Possible Is:

_____

_____

_____

_____

_____

_____

_____

_____

_____

_____

_____

_____

_____

_____

_____

_____

_____

_____

_____

_____

Forgiveness

I am Woman, therefore, I am forgiveness.
I am love. I am compassionate. I am empathetic. I am sympathetic. I am patient, I have mercy and I am merciful.
I am Woman and I am forgiveness. I am the love of God, the goodness of God, I display the grace of God.

I am Woman and I am one with all of humanity.
When I don't forgive others, I have not forgiven myself.
Forgiveness is fundamental to living a full, free, joyful, loving, and fulfilling life. Every unforgiving ounce that I harbor is a block to my own goodness, blessings, and joy.

I think of myself as a cup. If I'm using part of my cup (mental, spiritual, emotional space) to harbor unforgiveness, unforgiveness is then occupying precious real estate that God intended to be used for healing, encouragement, and the inspiration of others.

Not only will unforgiveness stop, stagnate, and impede my ability to empower others, it becomes the seed of regret and then regret becomes bitterness within myself.

The spirit of bitterness will ultimately have us become brittle.
Once we become brittle, we become hard, which means we've lost our vibrancy, our alive-ness. Brittleness dries our spirit and takes our luster, our joy, our creativity, our softness, our goodness,
and our love for humanity—the very thing God intended for us to be and do.
Forgiveness is fundamental.

TRUTH: TO THE EXTENT I'M WILLING TO FORGIVE, I AM FORGIVEN

I Am Woman, therefore, I Am Forgiveness:

_____

_____

_____

_____

_____

_____

_____

_____

_____

_____

_____

_____

_____

_____

_____

_____

_____

_____

Denying This Truth Has/Will Cost Me:

_____

_____

_____

_____

_____

_____

_____

_____

_____

_____

_____

_____

_____

_____

_____

_____

_____

_____

By Owning This Truth What Becomes Possible Is:

_____

_____

_____

_____

_____

_____

_____

_____

_____

_____

_____

_____

_____

_____

_____

_____

_____

_____

Choice

I am Woman, therefore, I am a choice.
I have options and I am the decider of those options.
I am Woman and every way that I am is a choice,
everything I do is a choice.

Even choosing not to choose is a choice. When God gave me the
gift of choice, He also built into me an inherent knowing of what
the best choices are for me.

However, there is a collective consciousness here on Earth that
sets the predetermined definition, roles, ideas, and meaning of
what it means to be Woman. This collective consciousness is
loud, powerful, mesmerizing, influential, and in many, many
ways, undermining of this gift and power of choice. In fact, the
message is, we as women don't get to choose. When indeed,
nothing could be further from the truth.

We are always at choice. We always have the right to choose,
the power to choose.
We simply must be willing to choose even when it makes those
around us uncomfortable. There is far too much at stake, to be
passive about our choices. To go along to get along is costly.

To silence our voice by not choosing to speak up,
shrinks us and robs us at our very core.
I am Woman, I have choice and I choose to choose.

TRUTH: IN WHAT I CHOOSE, I DEFINE

I Am Woman, therefore, I Have Choices:

_____

_____

_____

_____

_____

_____

_____

_____

_____

_____

_____

_____

_____

_____

_____

_____

_____

_____

_____

Denying This Truth Has/Will Cost Me:

_____

_____

_____

_____

_____

_____

_____

_____

_____

_____

_____

_____

_____

_____

_____

_____

_____

_____

_____

By Owning This Truth What Becomes Possible Is:

Unstoppable

I am Woman, therefore, I am unstoppable.

There's no force that compares to who God made me to be. I can't be contained.

I am relentless.

I am unwilling to yield, to give in, to give up.

When I am told I can't, I ask why not. When I am told I can't, my response is, I shall.

A common belief that the way to become unstoppable is not to stop, and the truth is, we have big dreams, big goals, and big vision. We will have big challenges, big breakdowns and often times, big discouragements. The key to being unstoppable is simply to keep getting up. What has us get up, is keeping the goal senior to the breakdown, the challenge, or the obstacle. Give the goal or the vision our power and focus. When we are discouraged and in breakdown, we tend to focus on the thing that stops us, versus resetting our focus on our vision.

Whatever you focus on is where your power will be. If you focus on the breakdowns, that's disempowering. If you refocus on the goal and the dream, it refuels, re-inspires, recharges us back up.

The bottom line, the way to become unstoppable is to simply keep getting up.

TRUTH: I AM UNSTOPPABLE

I Am Woman, therefore, I Am Unstoppable:

_____

_____

_____

_____

_____

_____

_____

_____

_____

_____

_____

_____

_____

_____

_____

_____

_____

_____

Denying This Truth Has/Will Cost Me:

_____

_____

_____

_____

_____

_____

_____

_____

_____

_____

_____

_____

_____

_____

_____

_____

_____

_____

_____

By Owning This Truth What Becomes Possible Is:

_____

_____

_____

_____

_____

_____

_____

_____

_____

_____

_____

_____

_____

_____

_____

_____

_____

_____

_____

Contribution

I am Woman, therefore, I am contribution and
I was born to contribute.

When I arrived on earth, I came with a message, a purpose, and a
reason for being. What also arrived with me was my assignment.

I've been given special gifts, talents, perspectives, and ideas, that
can shift, empower, influence, and change any situation or
circumstance. This privilege is not to be taken lightly.

When I withhold that which I am able to contribute, I am robbing
those around me and the world at large.

I am Woman. I stand and I contribute.

TRUTH: I STAND, I CONTRIBUTE

I Am Woman, therefore, I Contribute:

_____

_____

_____

_____

_____

_____

_____

_____

_____

_____

_____

_____

_____

_____

_____

_____

_____

_____

_____

Denying This Truth Has/Will Cost Me:

_____

_____

_____

_____

_____

_____

_____

_____

_____

_____

_____

_____

_____

_____

_____

_____

_____

_____

By Owning This Truth What Becomes Possible Is:

_____

_____

_____

_____

_____

_____

_____

_____

_____

_____

_____

_____

_____

_____

_____

_____

_____

_____

_____

_____

Possibilities

I am Woman, therefore, I am possibility.

At the center of who I am as Woman, is pure,
potent, unlimited possibility.

The Bible often speaks of,
"Morning by morning new mercies appear."

Morning by morning, when I awake, I am a blank canvas.

I am the painter. I hold the brush and the world is my oyster.
I can choose any color from the rainbow
to create the masterpiece called my life.

Given that I am pure possibility,
my resources are infinite, I am infinite.

TRUTH: MY POSSIBILITIES ARE ENDLESS

I Am Woman, therefore, I Am Possibilities:

_____

_____

_____

_____

_____

_____

_____

_____

_____

_____

_____

_____

_____

_____

_____

_____

_____

_____

Denying This Truth Has/Will Cost Me:

_____

_____

_____

_____

_____

_____

_____

_____

_____

_____

_____

_____

_____

_____

_____

_____

_____

_____

By Owning This Truth What Becomes Possible Is:

_____

_____

_____

_____

_____

_____

_____

_____

_____

_____

_____

_____

_____

_____

_____

_____

_____

_____

_____

Visionary

I am Woman, therefore, I am a visionary.
I am imaginative, ingenious, inventive, innovative, insightful,
perceptive, and driven.

I am futuristic. I can see possibilities and imagine and vividly see
things that others cannot see. As a visionary, I am a stimulator,
inspirer, motivator, and an influencer.

I am inquisitive and a challenger of the status quo, which opens up new
discoveries. Discovery is one of the most powerful things that exist.

Everything that is, once wasn't and how it all came to be, is due to a
visionary having pushed passed what is. What fit tradition and what
had already been done. It is the mind of the visionary that propels
life, as we know it, forward.

It is the mind of the visionary that annihilates the status quo and
leads us to advancements and new possibilities that would not exist.

When Steve Jobs was in the middle of discovering Mac, no one
could actually see it but him. It was so futuristic, even some of the
most brilliant minds he had around him could not conceive the
magnitude of his vision. Now, we live in an iWorld.

The visionary never stops envisioning what's possible. Surely Steve
Jobs could've stopped with the Mac, but he continued to push past
the current reality—iPhone, iPod, iPad, iWorld.

When a Woman has a vision and owns her power as a visionary,
humanity evolves.

TRUTH: I SEE FARTHER THAN I AM

I Am Woman, therefore, I Am A Visionary:

_____

_____

_____

_____

_____

_____

_____

_____

_____

_____

_____

_____

_____

_____

_____

_____

_____

_____

_____

Denying This Truth Has/Will Cost Me:

_____

_____

_____

_____

_____

_____

_____

_____

_____

_____

_____

_____

_____

_____

_____

_____

_____

By Owning This Truth What Becomes Possible Is:

_____

_____

_____

_____

_____

_____

_____

_____

_____

_____

_____

_____

_____

_____

_____

_____

_____

_____

Peace

I am Woman, therefore, I am peace.
I am free from disturbance, worry, fear, or doubt. I embody
tranquility. I move with ease and a knowing.

I am Woman. I have the peace and power of God. I am in
divine flow, there is nothing to resist.
I know all things, at all times are exactly as they should be.

I live and am at peace with all things because I know God loves
me, protects me, and cares for me. The very numbers of hairs on
my head are accounted for. I was intended for and God is
intentional, nothing is accidental, and it is God's intention that I
prosper, even that my soul prospers!

God request that I cast all my cares upon Him and
he shall carry them.
He will keep me from falling, even when I fall, I can't fail.

I Am Woman and I am intended to triumph.
No one and no circumstance can take me out of God's protective
care. God loves me, protects me, provides for me, and only wants
the very best for me.

I am a divine design, with a divine purpose and there is nothing or
no one that can stop my destiny.
I walk in Peace. I rest in the Peace of God, and I am Peace.

**TRUTH: NO FORCE IS MORE POWERFUL THAN
GOD'S LOVE FOR ME**

I Am Woman, therefore, I Am Peace:

_____

_____

_____

_____

_____

_____

_____

_____

_____

_____

_____

_____

_____

_____

_____

_____

_____

_____

Denying This Truth Has/Will Cost Me:

_____

_____

_____

_____

_____

_____

_____

_____

_____

_____

_____

_____

_____

_____

_____

_____

_____

_____

_____

_____

By Owning This Truth What Becomes Possible Is:

_____

_____

_____

_____

_____

_____

_____

_____

_____

_____

_____

_____

_____

_____

_____

_____

_____

Love

I am Woman, therefore, I am LOVE.

I am tender. I am warm. I am committed. I am understanding. I am patient. I am kind and generous. I am gentle, quick to listen and slow to speak, slow to find fault.

I am love and I am empowering. I am honest. I am considerate. I am love and I am flexible.

I am accommodating. I give myself a chance and I give others a chance. I look for and find the good in all circumstances and all people.

As love, I don't keep count. I don't point out faults and flaws in others. I don't break trust or gossip. I am love and I am not jealous, envious, back biting, pious, easily offended, or defensive.

I am love. I am the heart of God, the mind of God, the words of God, the spirit of God, the light of God, the beauty of God.

Love is the pure goodness of God. It elevates, reassures, empowers.

Love is power and powerful.

It is the greatest force there is. Love is God in action on Earth, Heaven, and beyond.

If you choose it, Love is You!

TRUTH: GOD IS LOVE, I AM ONE WITH GOD AND I AM LOVE

I Am Woman, therefore, I Am Love:

_____

_____

_____

_____

_____

_____

_____

_____

_____

_____

_____

_____

_____

_____

_____

_____

_____

_____

_____

_____

Denying This Truth Has/Will Cost Me:

_____

_____

_____

_____

_____

_____

_____

_____

_____

_____

_____

_____

_____

_____

_____

_____

By Owning This Truth What Becomes Possible Is:

_____

_____

_____

_____

_____

_____

_____

_____

_____

_____

_____

_____

_____

_____

_____

_____

_____

_____

_____

Fire

I am Woman, therefore, I am fire.

I am fire. I am able to ignite, start, and infuse energy.

I ignite ideas, brilliance, possibilities, dreams, and inventions in
all that I touch or come in contact with.

I am a catalyst.

I push and challenge those around me
while calling myself forward.

You cannot be in my presence and not feel the heat of new
possibilities, new ground being taken,
new experiences being unleashed.

I am Woman, I arouse, lift, move, and energize the world.

TRUTH: I AM WOMAN AND I AM FIRE

I Am Woman, therefore, I Am Fire:

_____

_____

_____

_____

_____

_____

_____

_____

_____

_____

_____

_____

_____

_____

_____

_____

_____

_____

_____

Denying This Truth Has/Will Cost Me:

_____

_____

_____

_____

_____

_____

_____

_____

_____

_____

_____

_____

_____

_____

_____

_____

_____

_____

_____

By Owning This Truth What Becomes Possible Is:

_____

_____

_____

_____

_____

_____

_____

_____

_____

_____

_____

_____

_____

_____

_____

_____

_____

_____

_____

_____

Abundant

I am Woman, therefore, I am abundant.
I am rich, lavish, bountiful, overflowing, infinite in exhaustible,
huge, and generous.

I am Woman. I am more than adequate. I am over sufficient.
There is no end to who I am and what I can achieve. I am
Woman. I determine the heights I can reach, the ideas I can
create, the dreams that I manifest.

My impact has an endless reach. There is no mountain too big to
climb, no challenge too great to conquer. I am Woman and I have
the resources I need to win and accomplish anything I set out to
achieve. There are over seven billion people on the planet and too
many to count that are willing to join forces with me in the
fulfillment of my dreams.

My resources are so plentiful that I serve as a resource for others.
The earth is inexhaustible and so am I.
I am one with the creator of all things, therefore, there is NO-
Thing that I cannot create.

I live in overflow, I am not part of the river, I am the river.
I am not part of the ocean, I am the ocean.
I am one with ALL there is, therefore, I am forever,
always and forever more.

I am abundant!

TRUTH: I AM PLENTIFUL

I Am Woman, therefore, I Am Abundant:

_____

_____

_____

_____

_____

_____

_____

_____

_____

_____

_____

_____

_____

_____

_____

_____

_____

_____

Denying This Truth Has/Will Cost Me:

_____

_____

_____

_____

_____

_____

_____

_____

_____

_____

_____

_____

_____

_____

_____

_____

_____

_____

_____

By Owning This Truth What Becomes Possible Is:

_____

_____

_____

_____

_____

_____

_____

_____

_____

_____

_____

_____

_____

_____

_____

_____

_____

_____

_____

Undaunted

———

I am Woman, therefore, I am undaunted.

I am courageously resolute, bold, steady, resolved, marked by determination in the face of life challenges and difficulties.

God has given me the power not to be daunted, dismayed, or diminished or reduced by the challenges of life.

When I become disconnected with these God-given gifts, I become disempowered.

By owning this truth of my undauntedness, no-thing is impossible. In fact, a life of freedom, joy, peace, and power become my context for living.

TRUTH: I AM WOMAN AND I AM UNDAUNTED

I Am Woman, therefore, I Am Undaunted:

_____

_____

_____

_____

_____

_____

_____

_____

_____

_____

_____

_____

_____

_____

_____

_____

_____

_____

Denying This Truth Has/Will Cost Me:

_____

_____

_____

_____

_____

_____

_____

_____

_____

_____

_____

_____

_____

_____

_____

_____

_____

_____

By Owning This Truth What Becomes Possible Is:

_____

_____

_____

_____

_____

_____

_____

_____

_____

_____

_____

_____

_____

_____

_____

_____

_____

_____

Unmatched

I am Woman, therefore, I am unmatched.

Fearless, unparalleled, incomparable, beyond comparison, limitless unique, exquisite, transcendent, superlative, outstanding, premier, rare, unexampled, unsurpassable and like none other.

When God made *Woman*, He broke the mold so that she could not be replicated. Such that she should not be defined by man, circumstances, and situations.

I am Woman and I am a force.

When God made me, He took a deep breath and marveled and His creation. God said you are beautiful, precious, and something to behold.

You are unmatched. You are the daughter of the Most High.

TRUTH: I AM WOMAN, UNMATCHED FEARLESS, AND A FORCE TO BE RECKONED WITH

I Am Woman, therefore, I Am Unmatched:

Denying This Truth Has/Will Cost Me:

_____

_____

_____

_____

_____

_____

_____

_____

_____

_____

_____

_____

_____

_____

_____

_____

_____

_____

By Owning This Truth What Becomes Possible Is:

_____

_____

_____

_____

_____

_____

_____

_____

_____

_____

_____

_____

_____

_____

_____

_____

_____

_____

_____

_____

_____

Unwavering

I am Woman, therefore, I am unwavering.

I shall not be moved.

I am unshakable, indefatigable, relentless,
vigilant and determined.

I am like a strong oak, a powerful redwood, whose roots run deep.
I am like a graceful palm. I have the flexibility to bend and sway,
but not to break.

I am like the thorns on a rose bush, sweet but prickly about my
worth and my truth.

I shall remember that I am steadfast, immeasurable, grounded in
the magnificence of who God designed me to be.

TRUTH: I AM WOMAN AND I AM UNWAVERING

I Am Woman, therefore, I Am Unwavering:

_____

_____

_____

_____

_____

_____

_____

_____

_____

_____

_____

_____

_____

_____

_____

_____

_____

_____

_____

_____

_____

_____

Denying This Truth Has/Will Cost Me:

_____

_____

_____

_____

_____

_____

_____

_____

_____

_____

_____

_____

_____

_____

_____

_____

_____

_____

By Owning This Truth What Becomes Possible Is:

_____

_____

_____

_____

_____

_____

_____

_____

_____

_____

_____

_____

_____

_____

_____

_____

_____

_____

Creator

I am Woman, therefore, I am creator.

The definition of creator is one who brings something into existence. As Woman, I am always creating. I am the creator of all my experience, love, life, and joy.

I am one with the Ultimate Creator. When I own that I am the source of all that I am creating, I get to determine the very fabric and essence of my life. I even create my own mindset.

I am responsible for my experiences and one with the Ultimate Creator.

If I were to be in complete alignment with the source and power that created me, which is also the power within me, there would be nothing that I could not create.

**TRUTH: I AM WOMAN, THEREFORE,
I AM CREATOR**

I Am Woman, therefore, I Am the Creator:

_____

_____

_____

_____

_____

_____

_____

_____

_____

_____

_____

_____

_____

_____

_____

_____

_____

_____

Denying This Truth Has/Will Cost Me:

_____

_____

_____

_____

_____

_____

_____

_____

_____

_____

_____

_____

_____

_____

_____

_____

_____

_____

By Owning This Truth What Becomes Possible Is:

_____

_____

_____

_____

_____

_____

_____

_____

_____

_____

_____

_____

_____

_____

_____

_____

_____

_____

_____

_____

Bold

I am Woman, therefore, I am bold.

I am daring, courageous, brave, fearless, audacious, spirited, positive, decisive, risky, assured, and enterprising. There is no challenge too big.

I am bold, therefore, I take the road less traveled.
If there is no road, I will create one.

I stand on the side of what's right when it's not popular.
When others say you can't, I ask why not?
When others say no, I say, yes I can.

I am willing to be the forerunner, the odd one, and the peculiar one. I take risks when there is no evidence that it can be done.

I am the embracer of what hasn't happen yet. I am Woman, I am fearless, and I know that the only thing to fear is fear itself.

The only thing to doubt is doubt.

The purpose for my existence is to create and manifest.

My purpose and to life fully and fulfilled.

TRUTH: I AM WOMAN AND I AM BOLD

I Am Woman, therefore, I Am Bold:

_____

_____

_____

_____

_____

_____

_____

_____

_____

_____

_____

_____

_____

_____

_____

_____

_____

_____

Denying This Truth Has/Will Cost Me:

By Owning This Truth What Becomes Possible Is:

_____

_____

_____

_____

_____

_____

_____

_____

_____

_____

_____

_____

_____

_____

_____

_____

_____

_____

Worthy

I am Woman, therefore, I am worthy.

I am valuable. I am deserving. I am exquisite.

I am special. I am priceless.

I am to be held in the highest honor. I am wonderfully made. I am perfect. Even my imperfections are as they should be.

I am a gift, I am to be cherished, adored, and admired.

I am Woman and I am something to truly behold.

In God's eyes, I am by far one of his most esteemed creations.

I am the daughter of the Most High and I am worthy.

TRUTH: THERE IS NONE LIKE ME

I Am Woman, therefore, I Am Worthy:

_____

_____

_____

_____

_____

_____

_____

_____

_____

_____

_____

_____

_____

_____

_____

_____

_____

_____

_____

Denying This Truth Has/Will Cost Me:

_____

_____

_____

_____

_____

_____

_____

_____

_____

_____

_____

_____

_____

_____

_____

_____

_____

_____

_____

By Owning This Truth What Becomes Possible Is:

_____

_____

_____

_____

_____

_____

_____

_____

_____

_____

_____

_____

_____

_____

_____

_____

_____

_____

Virtuous

———

I am Woman, therefore, I am virtuous.

I am upright, kind, honorable, and honest. I am divine.
I am excellence. I am light.

I stand true to my convictions. My north star is kindness, justice,
compassion, and empathy for all of humanity. I am a nurturer and
I have a heart for the suffering.

I am Woman and I am a bridge. As Woman, my responsibility is
to exalt, exhort, to lift, to empower.

I am Woman and I am here to make the world a better place and

to transfer the Love of God to all that I meet.

**TRUTH: I AM WOMAN AND I AM THE LIGHT
OF GOD**

I Am Woman, therefore, I Am Virtuous:

_____

_____

_____

_____

_____

_____

_____

_____

_____

_____

_____

_____

_____

_____

_____

_____

_____

_____

_____

_____

Denying This Truth Has/Will Cost Me:

_____

_____

_____

_____

_____

_____

_____

_____

_____

_____

_____

_____

_____

_____

_____

_____

_____

By Owning This Truth What Becomes Possible Is:

_____

_____

_____

_____

_____

_____

_____

_____

_____

_____

_____

_____

_____

_____

_____

_____

_____

_____

_____

_____

Unapologetic

I am Woman, therefore, I am unapologetic.

I am strong. I am proud. I am free of shame, guilt,
and apologies for who I am.

I am empowered to be me. I embrace, celebrate, and love myself
unconditionally. I love ALL of me, not just parts of me,
all of what makes me uniquely me.

I will not allow the world's opinions, other people's point of view,
beliefs, ideas, judgments, criticisms,
or even others' praises define me.

I shall only be defined by my values, my beliefs, my dreams, my
style, my principles, my truth. I will be my own judge and jury.

I will tread ever so lightly when I am judging myself.
I will give myself lots of grace.

I will move very aggressively when I am praising and
acknowledging the gift that I am and the gifts that I have.

I am Woman and I will dance my dance and sing my song.
I will write my story. I will create my life, my legacy, and my
reason for being.

I am Woman and I am always unapologetically me!

TRUTH: I AM WOMAN AND I AM A MASTERPIECE

I Am Woman, therefore, I Am Unapologetic:

_____

_____

_____

_____

_____

_____

_____

_____

_____

_____

_____

_____

_____

_____

_____

_____

_____

Denying This Truth Has/Will Cost Me:

_____

_____

_____

_____

_____

_____

_____

_____

_____

_____

_____

_____

_____

_____

_____

_____

_____

_____

_____

By Owning This Truth What Becomes Possible Is:

_____

_____

_____

_____

_____

_____

_____

_____

_____

_____

_____

_____

_____

_____

_____

_____

_____

_____

_____

_____

Faith

I am Woman, therefore, I am faith.

I have faith, complete trust, and confidence.

Conviction steeped deep in my heart and spirit is faith.

Faith is as important as the air I breathe. Just like oxygen nourishes the body, faith nourishes my heart, my soul, my mind.

Faith is the fuel that keeps me going. Faith empowers my dreams, it encourages me to take risk, to know that I can do anything, regardless of facts, circumstances, challenges, and disadvantages.

Faith propels me forward when logic says stop.

Faith gives me credibility with God! It has me knock on closed doors, ignore the closed sign, and apply for the loan, school, job. Faith propels me to go for it when man says I am not qualified.

Through faith, I know the word impossible does not apply to me and has no merit. There is no such thing as impossible.

Faith breeds the truth in my soul about who I really am: limitless, not to be contained, restricted, or denied.

I am a divine being, with a divine right to all that I can think, dream, or imagine.

TRUTH: A WOMAN'S FAITH TRANSCENDS FACTS

I Am Woman, therefore, I Am Faith:

_____

_____

_____

_____

_____

_____

_____

_____

_____

_____

_____

_____

_____

_____

_____

_____

_____

_____

_____

_____

Denying This Truth Has/Will Cost Me:

_____

_____

_____

_____

_____

_____

_____

_____

_____

_____

_____

_____

_____

_____

_____

_____

_____

_____

By Owning This Truth What Becomes Possible Is:

_____

_____

_____

_____

_____

_____

_____

_____

_____

_____

_____

_____

_____

_____

_____

_____

_____

_____

_____

_____

For additional information, visit
www.aiminghighinc.com.